Author Focus

Develop Your Author Vision Statement
and Laser-Focus Your Writing Career

WORKBOOK

By Christopher di Armani

Author Success Foundations Series Workbook 3

ISBN-13: 978-1988938189
ISBN-10: 198893818X

Editor: Nicolas Johnson

Published by

Botanie Valley Productions Inc.
PO Box 507
Lytton, BC V0K1Z0

https://BotanieValleyProductions.com
Sales@BotanieValleyProductions.com

Discover Your Path to Success

If you have not already done so, I recommend you read Author Focus: Develop Your Author Vision Statement and Laser-Focus Your Writing Career before you work through the exercises ahead.

https://ChristopherDiArmani.net/prolific-author

A vision statement describes your aspirations - the goals you hope to achieve - reflects your personal values, provides clarity and guides your decisions about current and future courses of action.

In short, a vision statement is your personal roadmap to success.

This process defines success for you. It defines excellence for you. It reflects your core beliefs and values. Most importantly, it spells out how you will live your life to achieve your goals.

As Lewis Carroll explained in Alice's Adventures in Wonderland, if you don't know where you're going, the road you choose does not matter.

> "*Cheshire Puss,*" Alice began, rather timidly, as she did not know whether it would like the name: however, it only grinned a little wider. "*Would you tell me, please, which way I ought to go from here?*"
>
> "*That depends a good deal on where you want to get to,*" said the Cat.
>
> "*I don't much care where,*" said Alice.
>
> "*Then it doesn't matter which way you go.*"

You cannot create your ideal future if you don't know what you want. You cannot reach your destination if you don't know where you're going.

This is an intensely personal process, a time of introspection and self-reflection. While the process is deeply inner-focused, its outcome reflects your values to the world and offers clarity to turn your dreams into reality.

A vision statement:

1. Combines every aspect of who you are
2. Gives you focus
3. Guides and simplifies your decisions
4. Holds you accountable for your decisions and actions
5. Acts as a unifying force for everything you do
6. Motivates and inspires you to achieve your writing goals

The importance of this for you, the writer, should be obvious. By knowing what you value and the ultimate goal for your writing life, you can focus your time and energy on the tasks to get you there. In so doing, you will arrive at your destination faster than you believe possible today.

Be Fearless

When you immerse yourself in this process with an honest and an open heart, you will uncover the three keys essential to your ideal future. Use those keys to construct the roadmap, the most direct path, to this future.

Shall we begin?

All men dream, but not equally. Those who dream by night in the dusty recesses of their minds wake in the day to find that it was vanity: but the dreamers of the day are dangerous men, for they may act their dream with open eyes to make it possible.

– T.E. Lawrence

Define Your Writing Dreams

Write down a list of all the things you want to write. When finished, rewrite it in order of priority.

With your list sorted in order of priority, define, as clearly as you can, the one thing you most want to write.

Why Do You Want To Write

What makes this project so important for you? Write down every reason why this is at the top of your list. Nothing is off limits.

To the best of your understanding, explain in clear language why you want to write this project.

Why Do You Hope To Accomplish?

A clear understanding of your personal motivation for writing this book will help drive you forward, even on the days you don't want to write. Every author writes for a variety of reasons. Every author is driven to write by different needs. Define, as clearly as possible, what you hope to accomplish by writing and publishing this book.

Goals Without Deadlines are Called Dreams

In the previous steps you defined what you want to write, why you want to write it and what you hope to accomplish with it. These are grand and important steps, but without a deadline they are meaningless. Setting a deadline brings your hopes and dreams into stark focus. Setting a deadline empowers you with a sense of urgency. That urgency powers you forward to take action.

The one and only restriction is your deadline must a date within 12 months of today.

My deadline for the first project on my list is ______________________________

What Must Happen for Your Writing to be Successful?

Writing success means something different for every writer. For some, it's financial independence. For others, it's helping a specific number of people accomplish a certain goal in their lives. For still others, it's delivering their message of hope to their target audience. Often it is a combination of these things.

For you to say, "I'm a successful writer" what must happen? Be precise.

What Are Your Dreams?

What are your biggest hopes and dreams?

Don't restrict your answer to writing. Fling open the doors of possibility and list every possible answer to the question "What do I want from my life?"

If Money Were No Obstacle, What Would You Do With Your Life?

Imagine today is ***Lottery Day*** and you just won a cool $100 million, tax free. If your money problems disappeared today, never to return, what would you do with your life? Where would you live? Who would live there with you? What would you do all day?

Close your eyes and picture, in your mind, your ideal life and all it entails. Write down what you see.

If You Knew You Could Not Fail What Would You Do?

Time to aim for the stars. If you knew success was 100% guaranteed, that you could not, for any reason, fail no matter what you decide to do, what would you do? Be specific. If you knew success was guaranteed, what would you do?

Honest Self-Evaluation - Tools for Success

For the past 12 months, identify the tasks, personality traits and systems you used to succeed. Which of these were most effective? Which helped you achieve a specific goal? The focus is on writing, but don't restrict yourself to just your writing successes. Include every tool you used to succeed this past year.

List Your Past Successes

In the previous section, you listed the systems, tools and personality traits you used to achieve success. In this section, you will list every success you achieved using them.

List Your Recent Failures

Nobody likes failure. We especially don't like examining our failures to see where we went wrong. List every failure of the past year. Beside each item on this list, write down what, if anything, you learned from this experience.

List Your Favorite Excuses

List your favorite excuses for not working, not writing or not accomplishing a goal. Then, with the completed list in front of you, beside each item, explain to yourself why this excuse has no basis in fact and what you will tell yourself instead to be responsible and accountable for your actions.

What Motivates You Best?

In a perfect world our best motivators would also be positive in nature, but sometimes the fear of a specific consequence is highly motivating. Are there things you fear, but find motivating?

Write down everything you find motivating, both positive and negative. When you're done, sort your list by its motivating factor in your life. What do you learn about yourself as a result of this exercise?

What Motivates You Least?

This is the reverse of the exercise you just completed. What attitudes and behaviors motivate you least? List everything that shuts off your motivation, be it an action or or attitude in yourself or others. How can you structure your life to avoid these things?

What Are Your Core Values?

Core values are your fundamental beliefs. They are the guiding principles for every decision you make in every area of your life. They dictate your behavior, often unconsciously, and form your moral compass - how you define right and wrong. From the list below, circle the values you identify with most powerfully.

Acceptance	Accomplishment	Achievement	Acknowledgement
Adaptability	Adventure	Affiliation	Ambition
Analytical	Appreciation	Approachability	Artfulness
Artistic Expression	Assertiveness	Assurance	Attentiveness
Authority	Autonomy	Availability	Balance
Beauty	Boldness	Bravery	Brilliance
Calmness	Care	Certainty	Challenge
Clarity	Cleverness	Comfort	Commitment
Community	Compassion	Competence	Competition
Complacency	Completion	Confidence	Connection
Consistency	Contemplative	Contentment	Contribution
Control	Conviction	Cooperation	Correctness
Courage	Creativity	Credibility	Cunning
Curiosity	Daring	Decisiveness	Delight
Dependability	Depth	Determination	Devotion
Directness	Discernment	Discipline	Discretion
Diversity	Duty	Education	Effectiveness
Emotional Health	Empathy	Encouragement	Enjoyment
Enthusiasm	Exactness	Excellence	Expediency
Experience	Expertise	Expressiveness	Facilitating
Fairness	Faith	Fame	Family-oriented
Fearlessness	Fidelity	Firmness	Fitness
Flexibility	Focus	Fortitude	Freedom
Friendly	Friendship	Frugality	Fulfilment
Fun	Generosity	Genuineness	Giving
Grace	Gratefulness	Gratitude	Growth
Guidance	Happiness	Hard working	Harmony
Health	Helpfulness	Heroism	High Earnings
Honest	Hospitality	Humility	Humor
Imagination	Impact	Independence	Industrious

Influence
Insightfulness
Inspiration
Integrity
Intelligence
Intimacy
Intuition
Inventiveness
Joy
Justice
Kindness
Knowledge
Leadership
Learning
Leisure
Logic
Love
Loyalty
Mastery
Maturity
Moderation
Nature
Openness
Optimism
Organization
Originality
Outgoing
Partnership
Passion
Peacefulness
Perfection
Perseverance
Persistence
Personal Growth
Personal Power
Persuasiveness
Playfulness
Pleasure
Positive
Predictability
Problem solving
Professionalism
Prosperity
Punctuality
Purity
Recognition
Recreation
Relaxation
Reliability
Resilience
Resourcefulness
Respect
Responsibility
Risk-Taking
Security
Self-Control
Self-Discipline
Self-Expression
Self-Reliance
Self-Restraint
Service
Significance
Simplicity
Sincerity
Spiritual
Spirituality
Spontaneity
Stability
Status
Strength
Structure
Success
Sufficiency
Teamwork
Tenacious
Thoroughness
Time
Timeliness
Trust
Trustworthy
Truth
Understanding
Uniqueness
Unity
Usefulness
Variety
Vision
Warmth
Wisdom
Wittiness

Find Your Seven Core Values

This is an extremely subjective exercise, so don't worry about right and wrong answers. There are none.

On the left side of the page, write down all the items you circled in the previous exercise.

On the right side of the page, sort those values in your order of personal preference.

Your Seven Core Values

Examine your sorted list on the previous page. Write down the top seven entries on your list below.

1. ______________________________
2. ______________________________
3. ______________________________
4. ______________________________
5. ______________________________
6. ______________________________
7. ______________________________

Re-examine your seven core values and the order you listed them. Is the order still correct? If not, resort your seven core values into their proper order below.

1. ______________________________
2. ______________________________
3. ______________________________
4. ______________________________
5. ______________________________
6. ______________________________
7. ______________________________

Cut your list to three and write them below.

1. ______________________________
2. ______________________________
3. ______________________________

These values drive your actions and behavior. In essence, they are the core of who you are - qualities you value most in yourself and others. Meditate upon these values and examine your life for how these values manifest in your thoughts, decisions and actions.

If You Died Today, What Would Be Your Biggest Regret

If you died today, what would be your single biggest regret?

Write Your Own Obituary

If you live the life you most want to live, how would others describe you after you're gone? Write your obituary the way you want to be remembered, knowing your best friend will read this at your funeral.

What is Inscribed on Your Tombstone?

If you live the life you most want to live, what will the inscription on your tombstone say?

What One Change Can You Make Today to Bring Your Vision to Life?

With your ideal life described by your obituary, what one change can you make in your life right now, today, to bring this vision of your ideal life closer to reality in the present? Define the one action you can take, right now, to bring you one step closer to achieving your dream.

Five Essential Elements of Your Personal Vision Statement

Your personal author vision statement must be:

1. Clear
2. Compelling
3. Concise
4. Written in the Present Tense
5. Focused on the Long-Term

For a complete discussion of these essential elements, please refer to Chapter 8 of "*Author Focus - How to Develop Your Personal Vision Statement and Advance Your Writing Career Beyond Your Wildest Dreams.*"

Your First Draft

Write down everything you discovered was important to you, why, and what you want to do to achieve it. Don't worry about order at this stage. We'll address priorities when you're done here.

Your Author Vision Statement - Write Your First Draft

Like all writing, rewriting is where the magic happens. It's as true for epic novels as it is for vision statements. Take everything you wrote on the previous page and sort it, give it an order so it makes sense to you.

Your Author Vision Statement - Refinement Draft

Cut your author vision statement down to a single paragraph.

Your Author Vision Statement - Final Draft

As discussed previously, your author vision statement must be:

1. Written down.
2. No more than two sentences long.
3. Written so a ten-year-old child can understand it.
4. A statement you can (and will) recite from memory every morning to start your day.
5. The unique description of who you are and what values are most important to you.
6. A unique statement defining your life's priorities.
7. A unique plan of action for achieving your goals.

The final, polished draft of your author vision statement should be no more than 100 words. If you can write it down in half that, so much the better. Points are for brevity, clarity of purpose, motivation and action.

Power Points

Nothing proves your motivation more than your actions. Writing a book means taking action. Pretty simple, right? The following steps help you find ways to take action today.

Step 1. Identify your primary strength and list all the ways you can put that strength to work today to achieve success. How can you change your writing process to use your primary strength more often, to achieve even greater success using it?

Step 2. Identify one more strength you can put to work today, and continue to do more often, to support your personal sense of achievement.

Power Points

Step 3. What is the one thing you can do today, and do with greater frequency, to bring more joy to your life?

I am So Proud of You!

I congratulate you for your courage and tenacity. You finished an exercise most human beings will never even attempt. This is a massive accomplishment, so pat yourself on the back. You earned it!

Step back and admire your vision for your ideal future, then perform every task required to breathe life into your dream until it becomes your reality.

Then share your bold vision with the world.

The Bible, in Luke 14, verse 28, exhorts us to "count the cost."

> For which of you, intending to build a tower, does not sit down first and count the cost, whether he has enough to finish it; lest, after he has laid the foundation, and is not able to finish, all who see it mock him, saying, 'This man began to build and was not able to finish.'

To achieve your ideal life you must count the cost of achievement, then work hard every day to pay that price. You must build your personal tower of success. You must count the full cost of your published book in time, talent, skill development and treasure, and pay this price daily until you achieve your goal.

There is no other way.

If an easier path existed, everyone would write and publish a book.

They don't.

You will.

Next Steps

Success matters. The road you travel to achieve success matters even more.

Becoming an unstoppable writer is the natural outflow of fulfilling your core needs, but you still require structure to build your habits upon to guarantee your success. A daily routine, tailored to the wants, needs and commitments of your life, is essential to the fastest and shortest journey down Publication Highway.

Every writer's life is different. Your ideal daily writing routine is different than mine, and for good reason. You aren't me. Our lives differ, maybe a little, maybe by orders of magnitude. Who knows? Who cares? Our differences don't matter nearly as much as our similarities do.

Prolific Author - The Step-by-Step Guide to Write More Words in Less Time and Finish Your Book Fast uncovers those similarities, but only when you take action, when you complete the exercises with complete honesty.

Learn how to create a system, a daily writing routine, designed to push you forward to your goal. Follow this system and I guarantee you will finish your book and publish it, too.

Available from your favorite online book retailers today.

For more information, visit:

https://ChristopherDiArmani.net/prolific-author

Next Steps

www.ingramcontent.com/pod-product-compliance
Lightning Source LLC
LaVergne TN
LVHW061205120826
845149LV00011B/1914

* 9 7 8 1 9 8 8 9 3 8 1 8 9 *